"Enter the magical world of colors and imagination with my coloring book for children, where every page is an invitation to explore and create!"

I am grateful to God for everything!! And I believe that the meaning of life is to give meaning to other lives and you are the meaning of my life!!